THE FALL FEASTS

Activity Book for Beginners

The Fall Feasts Activity Book for Beginners

All rights reserved. By purchasing this Activity Book, the buyer is permitted to copy the activity sheets for personal and classroom use only, but not for commercial resale. With the exception of the above, this Activity Book may not be reproduced in whole or in part in any manner without written permission of the publisher.

Bible Pathway Adventures® is a trademark of BPA Publishing Ltd.

ISBN: 978-1-98-858536-9

Author: Pip Reid

Creative Director: Curtis Reid

For free Bible resources including coloring pages, worksheets, puzzles and more, visit our website at:

www.biblepathwayadventures.com

 # Introduction for Parents

Your children will LOVE learning about the Fall Feasts with *The Fall Feasts Activity Book for Beginners*. Packed with coloring pages, worksheets, crafts and puzzles to help educators just like you teach children the Biblical faith. Includes scripture references for easy Bible verse look-up. The perfect discipleship resource for Sabbath and Sunday School lessons, and homeschooling.

Bible Pathway Adventures® helps educators teach children the Biblical faith in a fun and creative way. We do this via our illustrated storybooks, Activity Books, and printable activities - available for download on our website www.biblepathwayadventures.com

Thanks for buying this Activity Book and supporting our ministry. Every book purchased helps us continue our work providing free Classroom Packs and discipleship resources to families and missions around the world.

The search for Truth is more fun than Tradition!

Table of Contents

Day of Trumpets (Yom Teru'ah)
Coloring page: Day of Blowing...6
Worksheet: Trace the Words 7
Connect the dots: A shofar!..8
Worksheet: I spy!...9
Let's learn Hebrew: Yom Teru'ah..10
Labyrinth: Where's my shofar?...12
Worksheet: Parts of a ram..13
Worksheet: Yah's calendar..14
Bible word search puzzle: Day of Trumpets 15
Worksheet: The number seven..16
Coloring page: The Sabbath 17
Worksheet: What's different?...18
Bible craft: Make a shofar 19
Let's learn Hebrew: Shofar 20
Worksheet: Alphabet challenge...22

Day of Atonement (Yom Kippur)
Coloring page: Yom Kippur...23
Coloring page: The High Priest...24
Tracing map: Help the High Priest find the temple..25
Finish the picture: The High Priest 26
Coloring page: What is repentance?..27
Let's learn Hebrew: Yom Kippur...28
Worksheet: Who entered the holy of holies?...30
Worksheet: The number 10..31
Worksheet: What a lot of animals!..32
Worksheet: T is for tribe...33
Worksheet: What's my sound?..34
Coloring page: Twelve tribes of Israel 35
Worksheet: Matching pairs 36
Bible activity: Dress like an Israelite..37

Feast of Tabernacles & The Last Great Day (Sukkot & Shemini Atzeret)
Coloring page: Sukkah for Sukkot 38
Worksheet: How did the Israelites travel? 39
Let's learn Hebrew: Sukkot 40
Tracing map: Help the Israelites get to Jerusalem 42
Map activity: Journey to Jerusalem 43
Bible word search puzzle: Sukkot 44
Worksheet: Days of the week 45
Worksheet: I spy! 46
Coloring page: Happy Sukkot! 47
Coloring page: Draw your own sukkah 48
Worksheet: S is for Sukkot 49
Connect the dots: King Solomon's temple 50
Labyrinth: The water ceremony 51
Worksheet: Trace the Words 52
Worksheet: W is for water 53
Coloring page: Are you thirsty? 54

Crafts & projects
Bible craft: Make a crown for a king! 57
Flashcards: Yom Teru'ah 61
Bible craft: The High Priests breastplate 63
Bible activity: The temple 65
Bible craft: Make a Yom Kippur necklace 67
Flashcards: Yom Kippur 71
Bible activity: The Israelites 73
Worksheet: Complete the pattern 75
Worksheet: Grapes and olives 77
Flashcards: Sukkot 79
Worksheet: The water ceremony 81
Bible craft: Make a Fall Feasts door hanger 83

Discover more Activity Books! 88

🌿 Day of Blowing 🌿

Trace the words. Color the picture.

day of blowing

Trace the Words

Color the pictures.

🐚	shofar
🐏	ram
👑	king
🕎	Yeshua

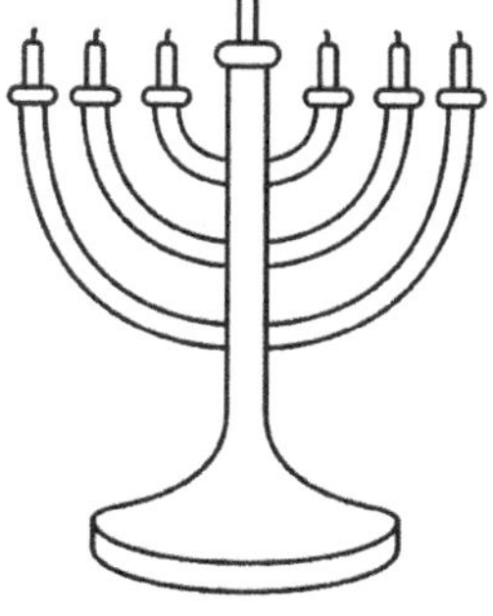

🌿 A shofar! 🌿

A shofar is made from a ram's horn. Connect the dots to see the picture.

I spy!

Yah told the Israelites to remember the Day of Trumpets forever. Color the same object a single color. Then count each type of object and write the number on the label.

Yom Teru'ah

The Hebrew words for Day of Trumpets are Yom Teru'ah.
The Israelites often anointed kings on this day.

yom teru'ah

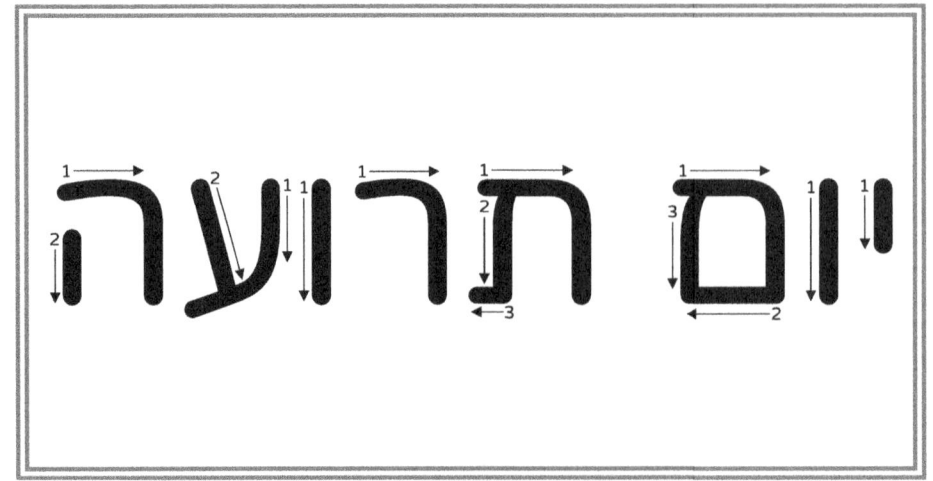

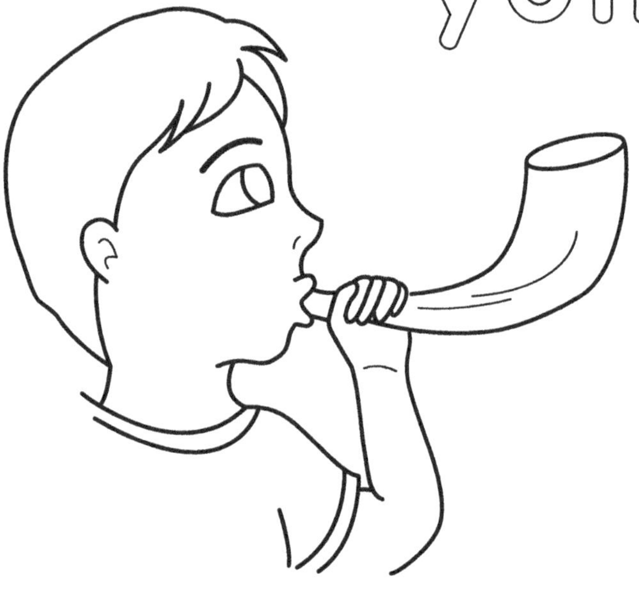

יום תְרוּעָה

Day of Trumpets

יום תרועה

 # Let's write!

Practice writing these Hebrew words on the lines below.

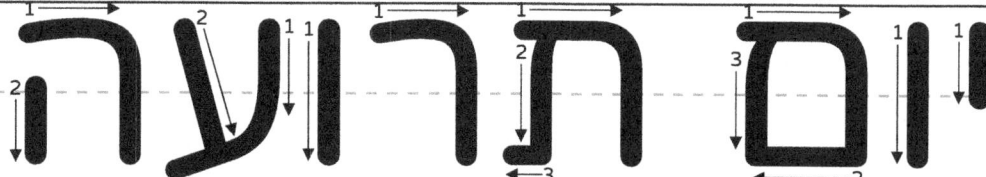

Try this on your own.
Remember that Hebrew is read from RIGHT to LEFT.

Where's my shofar?

Help the shofar blower find his shofar.

🌿 Parts of a ram 🌿

The Israelites made shofars out of a ram's horns.
Can you name the parts of a ram?

- ear
- eye
- mouth
- horn
- leg

Yah's calendar

Yah uses the sun, moon, and stars to tell us His plans and Appointed Times. Trace and color the pictures.

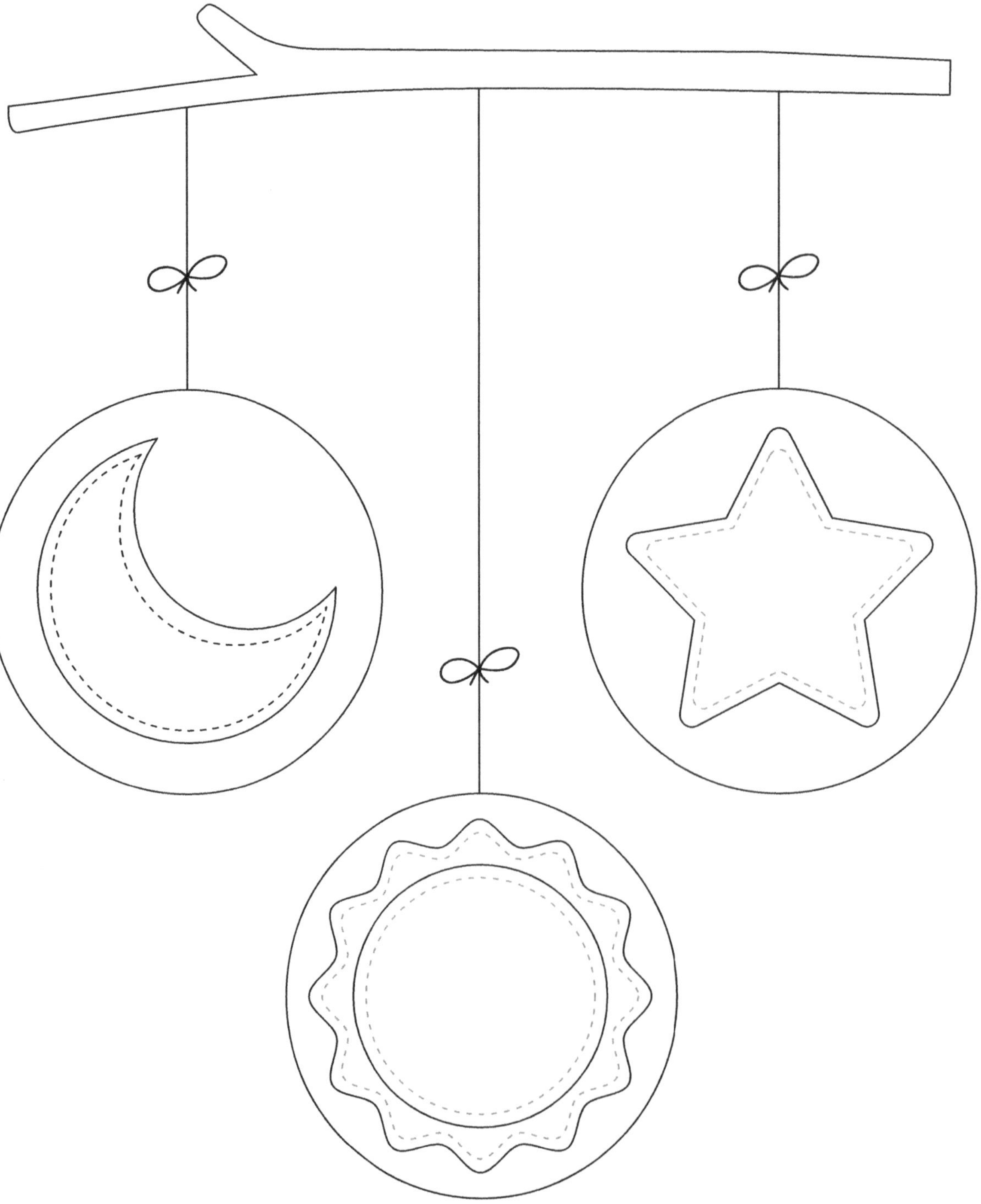

Day of Trumpets

Find and circle each of the words from the list below.

```
B X D T K H
Z L E P I O
O P O P N R
R A M W G N
S E V E N H
S H O F A R
```

KING   SHOFAR
BLOW   RAM
HORN   SEVEN

 # seven

The Day of Trumpets takes place in the 7th month (Tishrei 1).

Write the number seven in the boxes below.

How many fingers are there?

How do you celebrate the Day of Trumpets?

The Sabbath

The Day of Trumpets is a Sabbath (Leviticus 23). The Sabbath is day of rest for Yah's people.

🍃 What's different? 🍃

Circle the picture that is different.

Make a shofar

The Day of Trumpets means 'the day of the shofar blast' in Hebrew. Let's make a shofar!

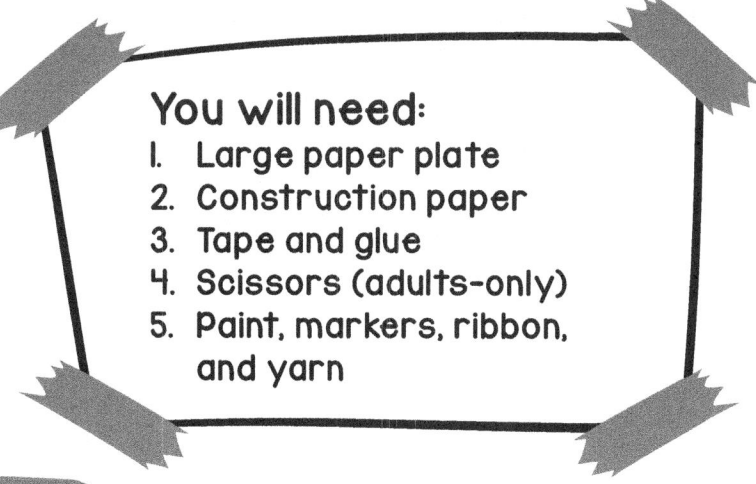

You will need:
1. Large paper plate
2. Construction paper
3. Tape and glue
4. Scissors (adults-only)
5. Paint, markers, ribbon, and yarn

Instructions:

1. Roll a large paper plate into a cone shape. Fasten with tape.
2. Glue construction paper around the cone shape. Use markers, ribbon or paint to decorate your 'shofar'.
3. Thread a piece of yarn through the inside of your shofar. Tie the ends to make a handle.

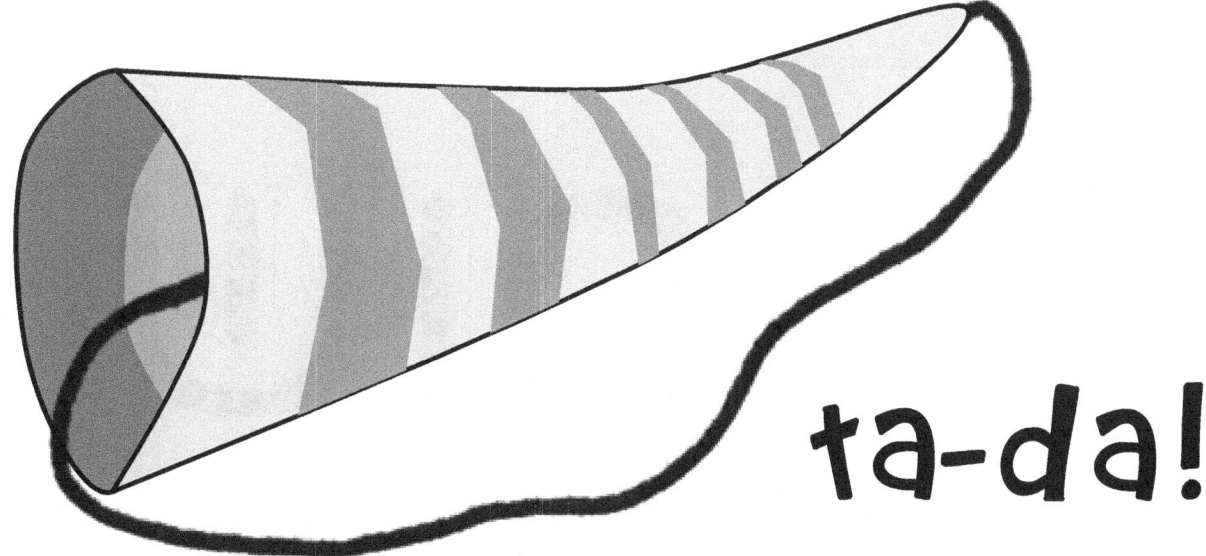

ta-da!

✶ Shofar ✶

The Hebrew word for trumpet is shofar. A shofar is made from a ram's horn and is blown on important days like the Day of Trumpets.

shofar

שׁוֹפָר

trumpet

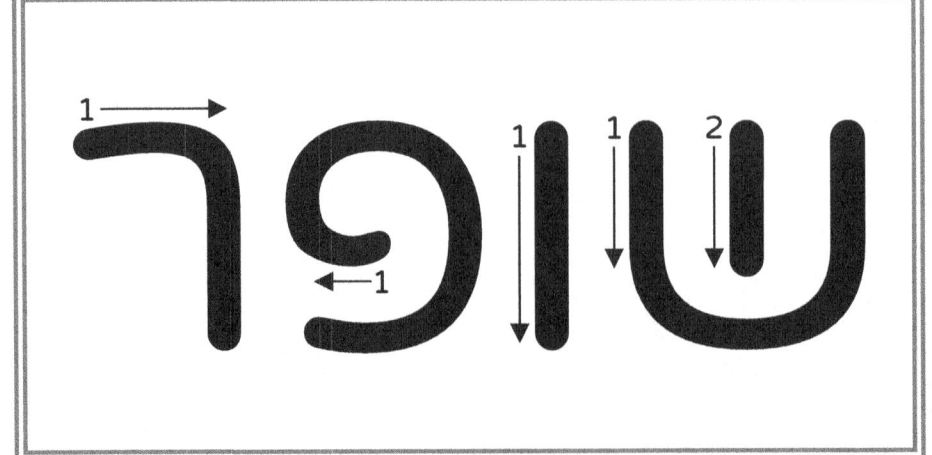

Let's write!

Practice writing this Hebrew word on the lines below.

שופר

שופר

Try this on your own.
Remember that Hebrew is read from RIGHT to LEFT.

The High Priest

Color the hat white. Color the robe blue.

The High Priest

Help the High Priest find the temple by tracing along the line.

🌿 Finish the picture

Color the picture and trace the word to find out who went into the Holy of Holies on Yom Kippur.

🌿 What is repentance? 🌿

Repentance is turning back to Yah and doing things His way instead of our own way. Color the picture.

Yom Kippur

The Hebrew words for Day of Atonement are Yom Kippur. On this day, the High Priest went into a special room in the temple called the Holy of Holies.

Let's write!

Practice writing these Hebrew words on the lines below.

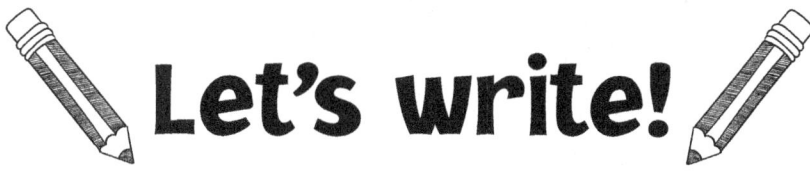

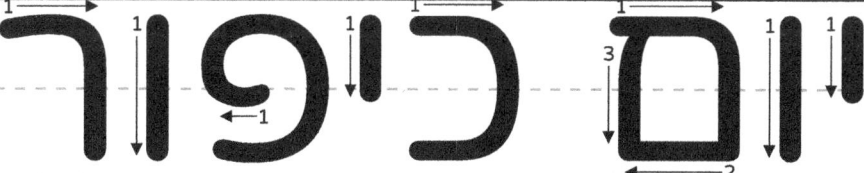

Try this on your own.
Remember that Hebrew is read from RIGHT to LEFT.

Yom Kippur

Who went inside the Holy of Holies on Yom Kippur?
Fill in the blanks using the chart below.

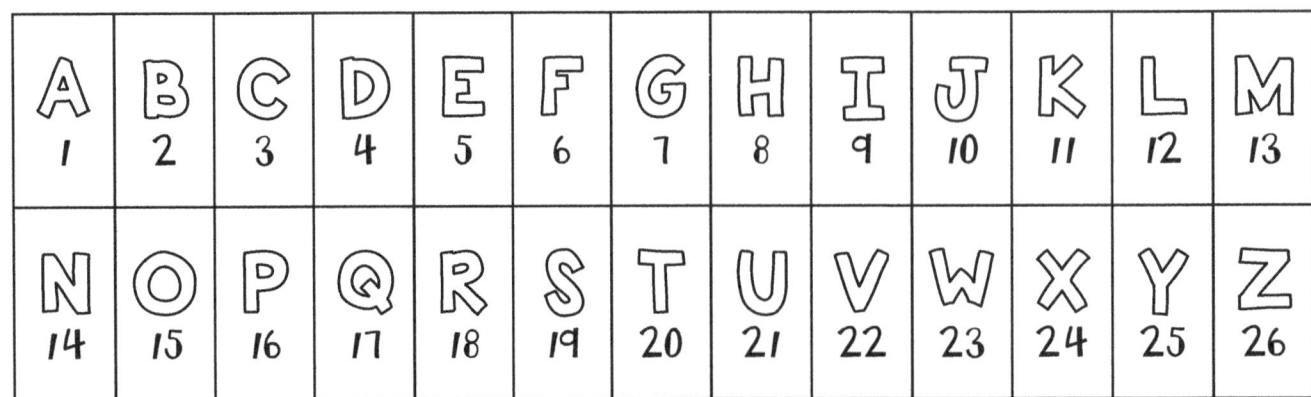

__ __ __ __ __ __ __
20 8 5 8 9 7 8

__ __ __ __ __ __
16 18 9 5 19 20

Speech bubble: What do you do on Yom Kippur?

A	B	C	D	E	F	G	H	I	J	K	L	M
1	2	3	4	5	6	7	8	9	10	11	12	13
N	O	P	Q	R	S	T	U	V	W	X	Y	Z
14	15	16	17	18	19	20	21	22	23	24	25	26

The Number 10

Yom Kippur is on the 10th day of the Hebrew month of Tishrei. Trace the numbers. Circle and color the animals.

Circle 10 goats

Color 10 bulls

What a lot of animals!

The Israelites gave burnt offerings to Yah on Yom Kippur (7 sheep, a goat, a ram, and a bull). Can you count all the animals?

T is for tribe

Yah asked the 12 tribes of Israel to honor Yom Kippur (Leviticus 23:2). Trace the letters. Color the picture.

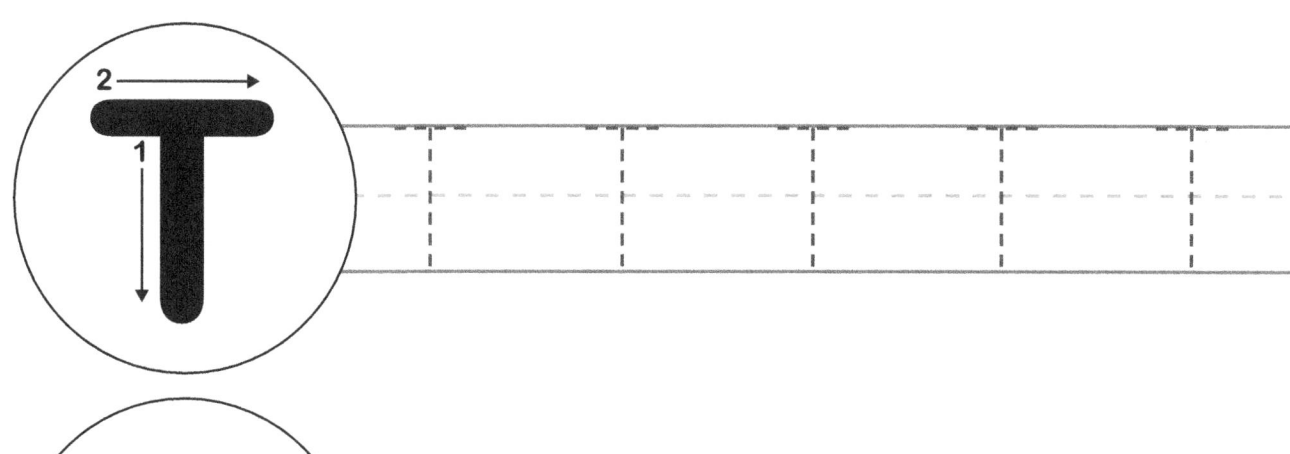

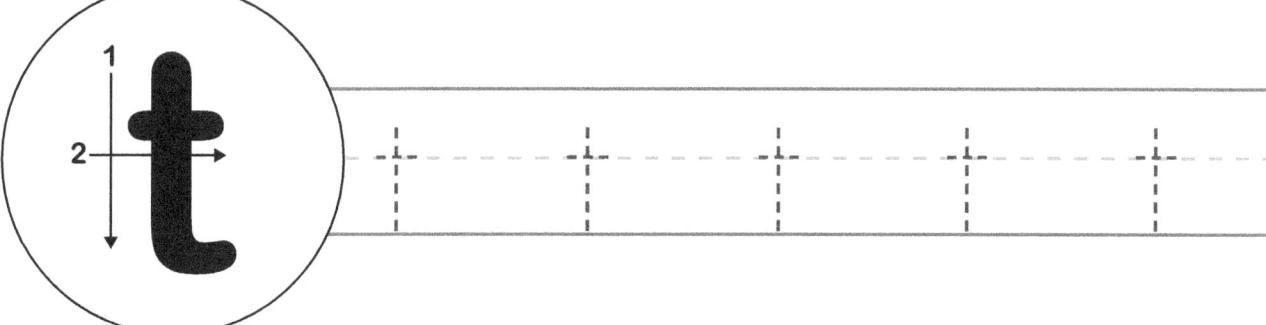

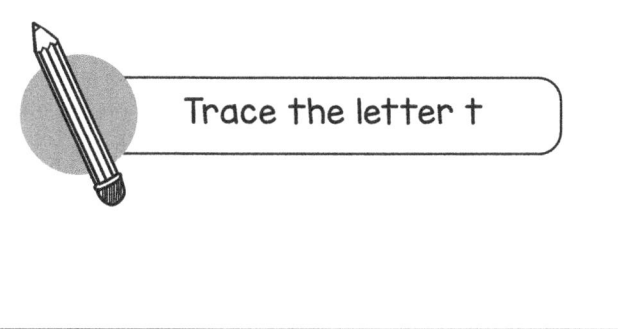

Trace the letter t

Color the commandments

What's my sound?

Yeshua is our High Priest. The word 'priest' starts with the letter p. Circle and color the pictures that start with the same beginning sound as priest.

bread

lamp

lion

pizza

plant

Twelve Tribes of Israel

The High Priest wore a special breastplate of gemstones. Each stone had the name of one of the 12 tribes of Israel. Color the picture.

Matching pairs

Draw a line between the matching objects.
Color the matching objects the same way.

🌿 Dress like an Israelite 🌿

The ancient Israelites wore clothing like tunics and robes. Let's make a tunic! Ask your parents to help you do this.

Instructions:

1. Parents - measure your child's body from elbow to elbow and knee to shoulder.
2. Find an old blanket or sheet as big as your child and fold it in half.
3. Cut a slit in the middle of the fold wide enough to fit their head.
4. Place the 'tunic' over their head. Tie a belt made from rope, ribbon, leather, or cloth around their waist.

1.   2.   3.   4.

ta-da!

Sukkah for Sukkot

During the Feast of Tabernacles (Sukkot), Israelites live in huts called sukkahs. Color the picture.

How did the Israelites travel?

Color the objects and animals that took the Israelites from one place to another.

Sukkot

The Hebrew word for Feast of Tabernacles is Sukkot.
It's a wedding feast!

sukkot

סֻכּוֹת

Feast of Tabernacles

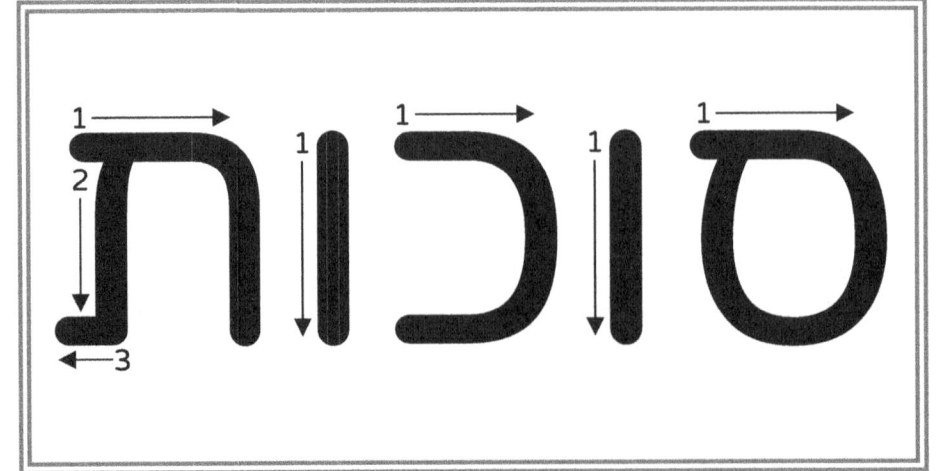

Let's write!

Practice writing this Hebrew word on the lines below.

סוכות

סוכות

Try this on your own.
Remember that Hebrew is read from RIGHT to LEFT.

🌿 The Israelites 🌿

Trace along the lines to help the Israelites get to Jerusalem to celebrate Sukkot.

Journey to Jerusalem

Every year, Israelites from many places came to Jerusalem to celebrate Sukkot. Draw a line from each place to Jerusalem to see their travels.

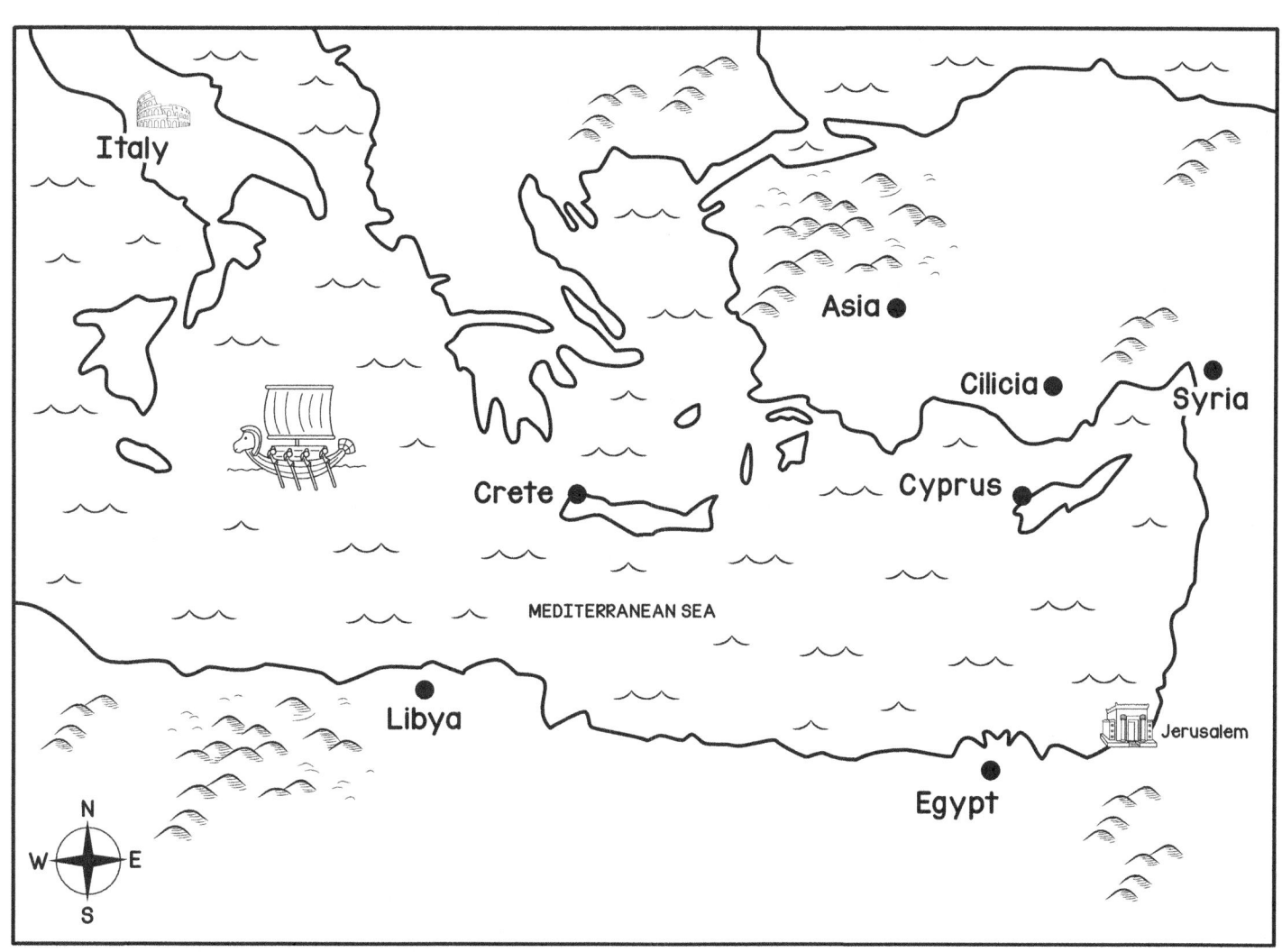

Sukkot

Find and circle each of the words from the list below.

```
I S R A E L
S U K K A H
W A T E R J
G H V M S A
T E N T L R
B R A N C H
```

TENT   SUKKAH
WATER   JAR
ISRAEL BRANCH

Days of the Week

The Feast of Tabernacles (Sukkot) lasts one week.
A week has seven days.
Fill in the letters to write the days of the week.

SUN D A Y   THURS __ __ __

MON __ __ __   FRI __ __ __

TUES __ __ __   SATUR __ __ __

WEDNES __ __ __

I spy!

During Sukkot, the Israelites liked to celebrate with music. Color the same instrument a single color. Count each type of instrument and write the number on the label.

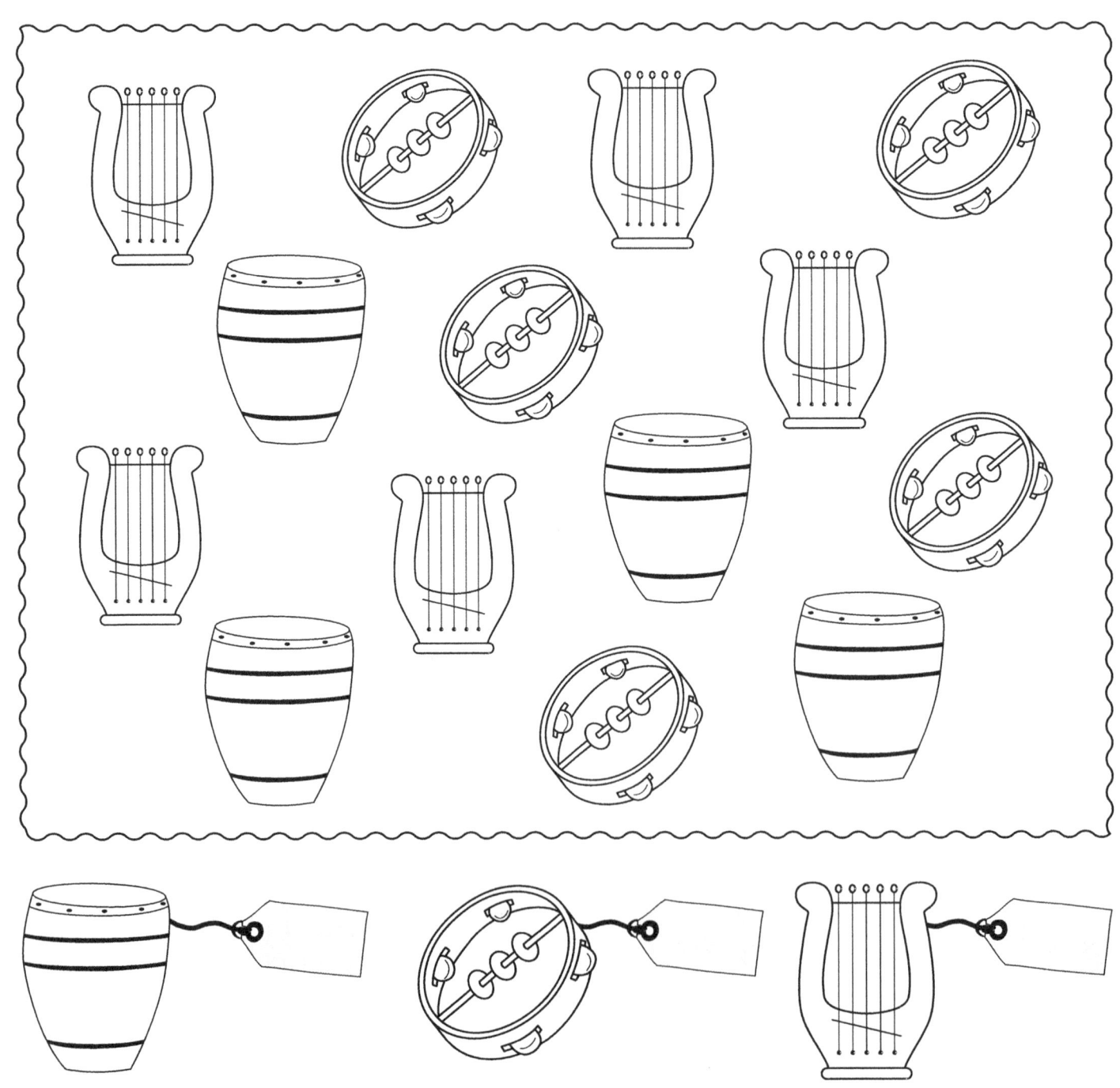

Let's Draw!

Draw your own Sukkah in the space below.

S is for Sukkot

Trace the letters and words. Color the picture.

S is for Sukkot

Connect the dots

King Solomon dedicated the temple to Yah during Sukkot. Connect the dots to see the temple. Color the picture.

The water ceremony

Help the priests take a jar of water back to the temple.

Start here!

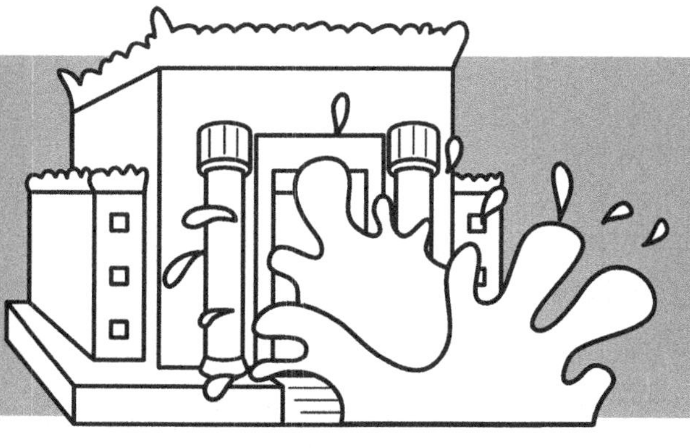

Trace the Words

Color the pictures.

⭐ W is for water ⭐

is for

water

"If anyone is thirsty, let him come to Me and drink..."

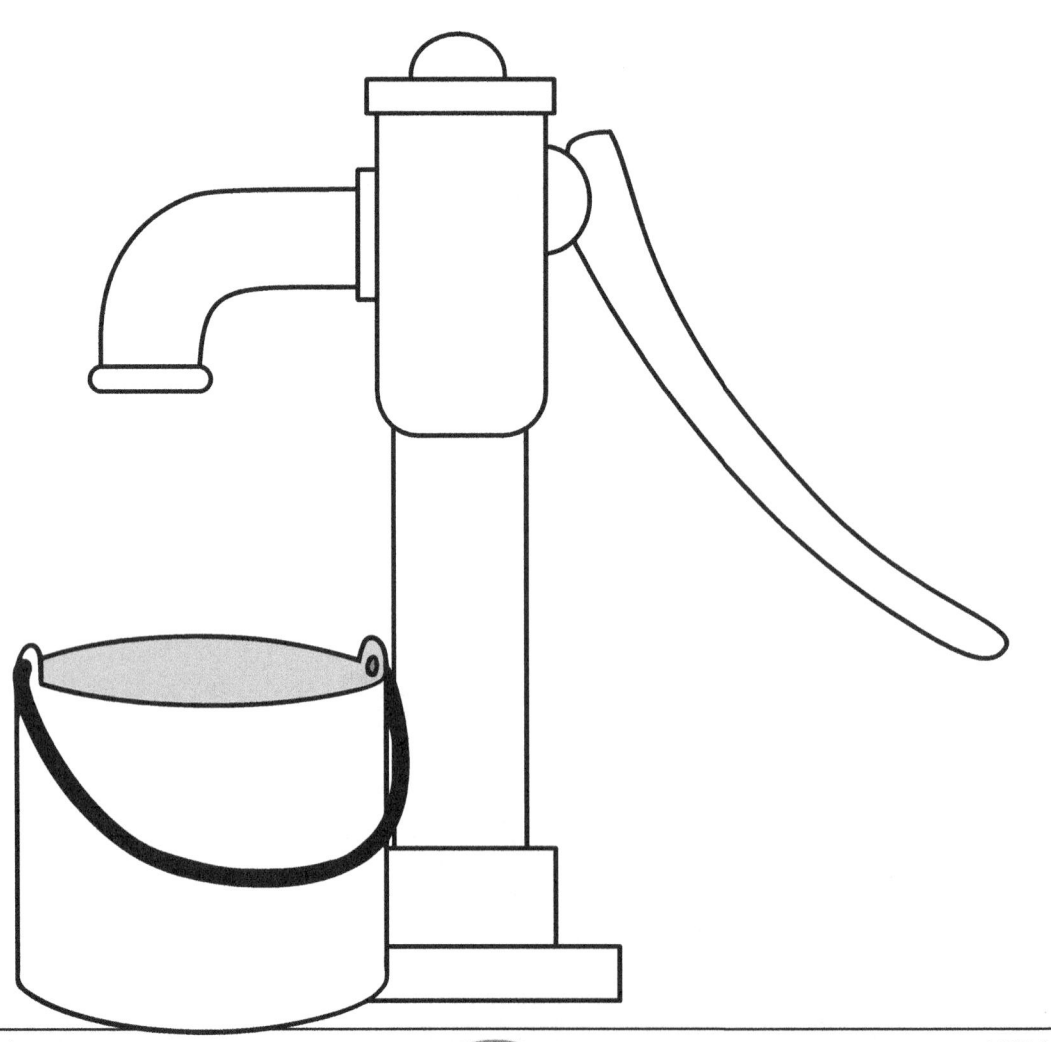

CRAFTS & PROJECTS

Make a crown for a king!

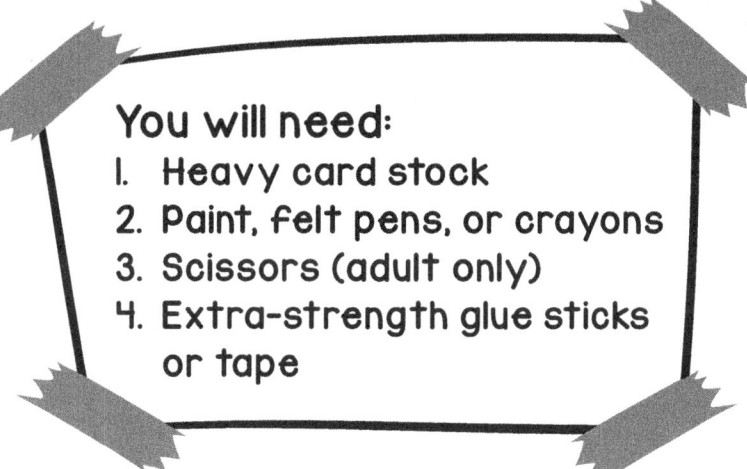

You will need:
1. Heavy card stock
2. Paint, felt pens, or crayons
3. Scissors (adult only)
4. Extra-strength glue sticks or tape

Instructions:

1. Cut out the crown and long rectangles on the next page.
2. Ask your child to decorate their crown however they like.
3. When they have finished decorating their crown, glue the long strips of paper to the sides of the crown.
4. Measure your child's head and glue into a crown. Use a glue stick or tape to do this.

Yom Teru'ah flashcards

Color and cut out the flashcards.
Tape them around your home or classroom!

High Priest's Breastplate

Color and cut out the breastplate. Thread a string through the four holes. Ask someone to tie the breastplate on you.

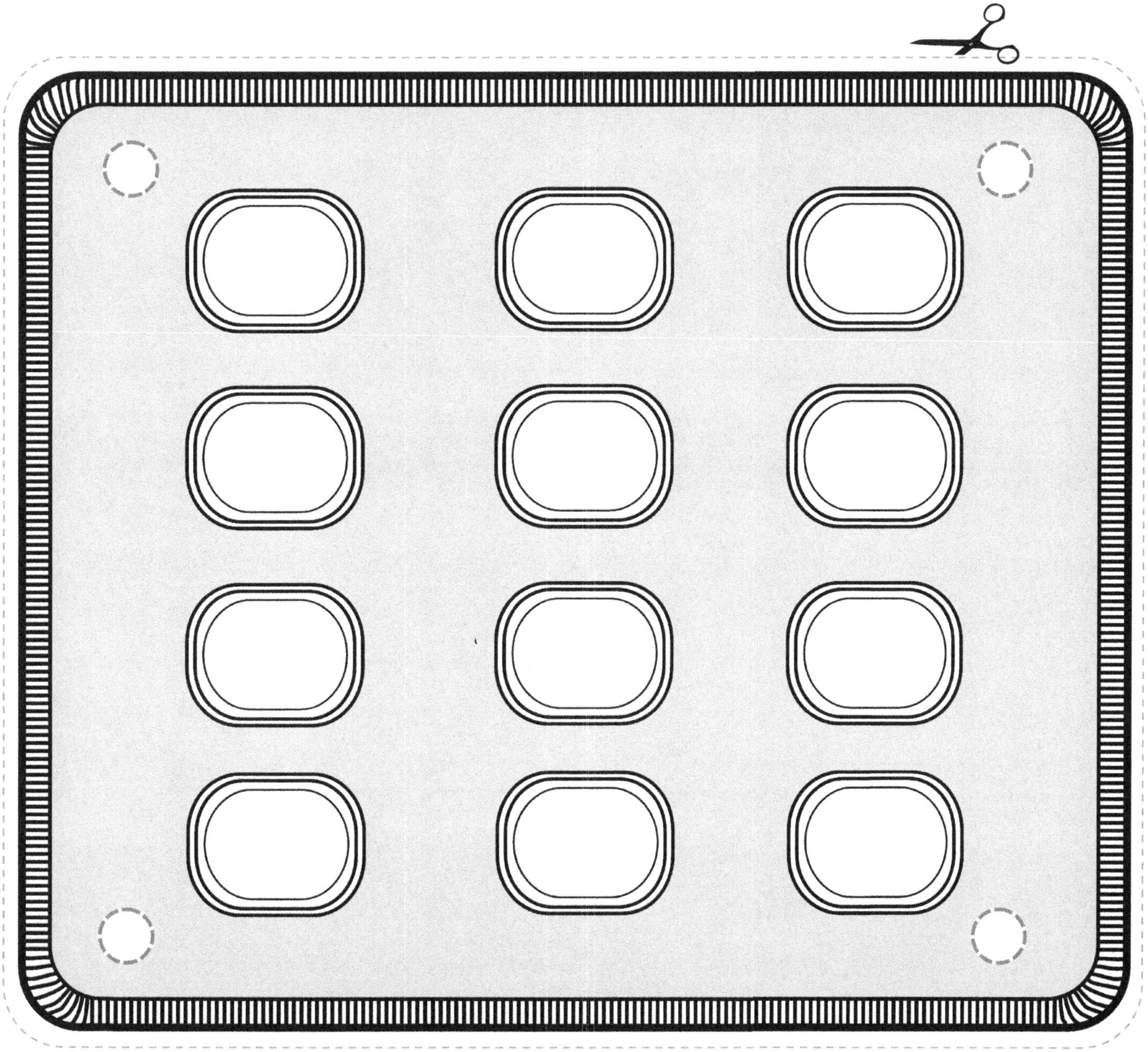

The temple

On Yom Kippur, the High Priest went into a special room in the temple called the Holy of Holies. Cut out the High Priest and objects. Place them in the temple.

High Priest  | **Menorah**  | **Torah**

Make a Yom Kippur necklace

You will need:
1. Yom Kippur pictures (see next page)
2. Paint, felt pens, or crayons
3. Scissors or hole punch
4. Yarn or string

Instructions:

1. Have your children color the pictures from Yom Kippur.
2. Cut out the pictures (children may need to help with this step).
3. Use a hole punch or scissors to create a hole in each of the circles.
4. String the circles with yarn or string to create a Yom Kippur necklace.

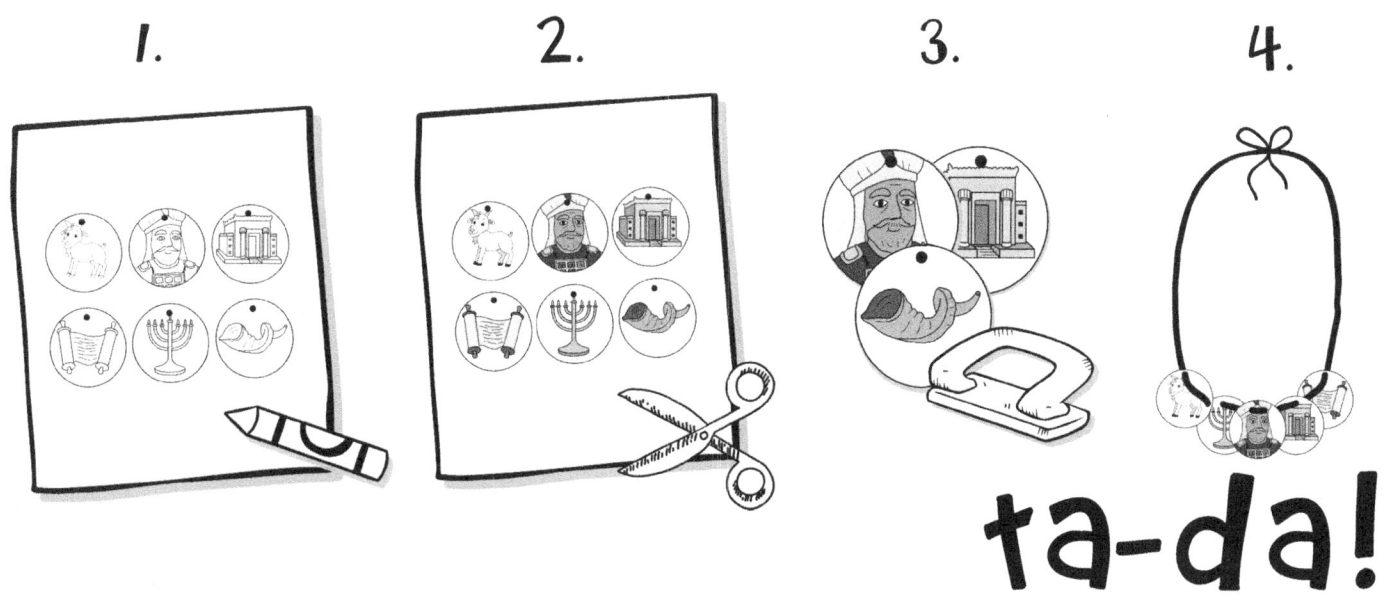

ta-da!

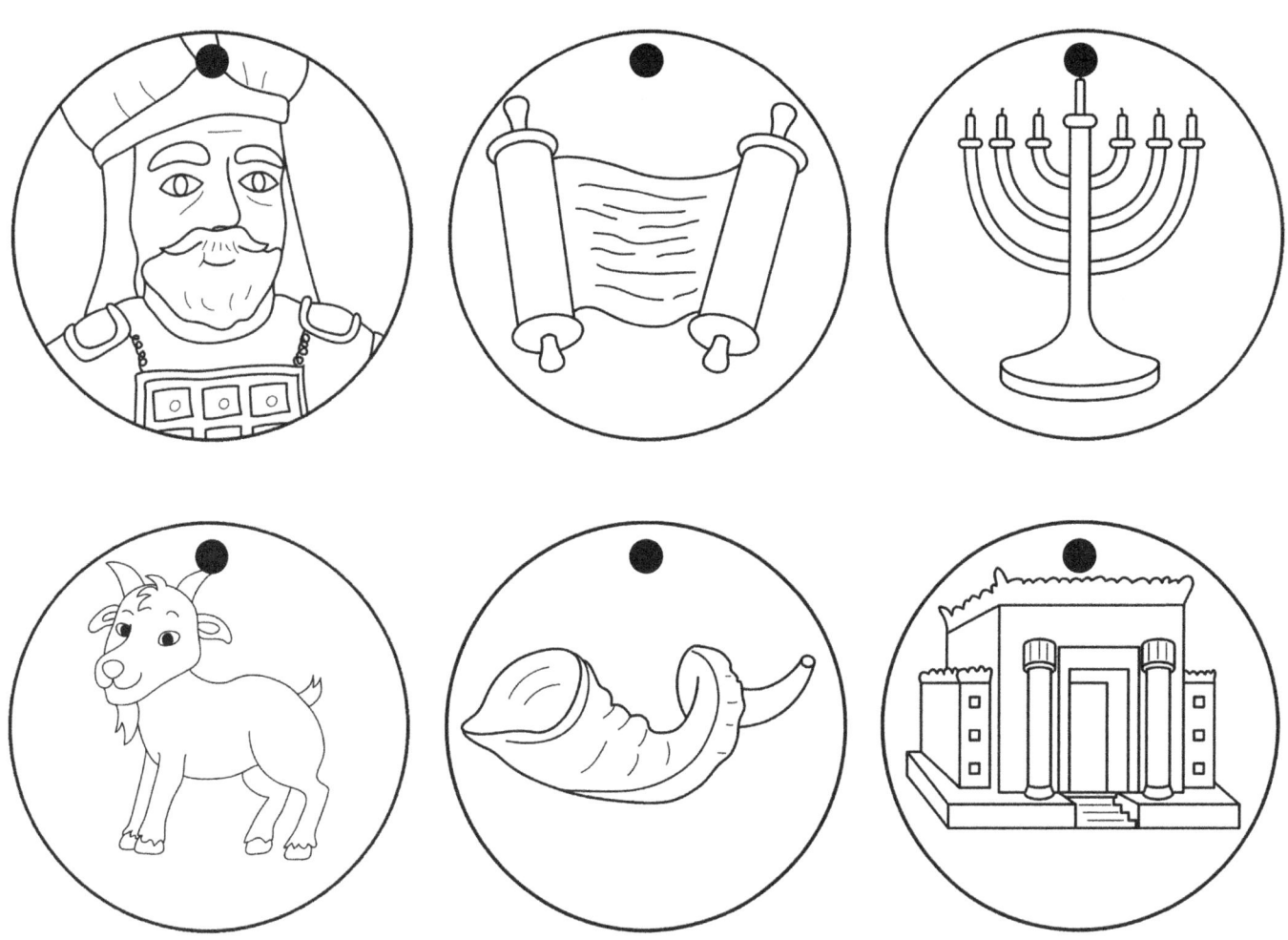

Yom Kippur flashcards

Color and cut out the flashcards.
Tape them around your home or classroom!

The Israelites

When the Israelites came to Jerusalem for Sukkot, they lived in tents outside the city. Color and cut out the people. Place them inside the tent.

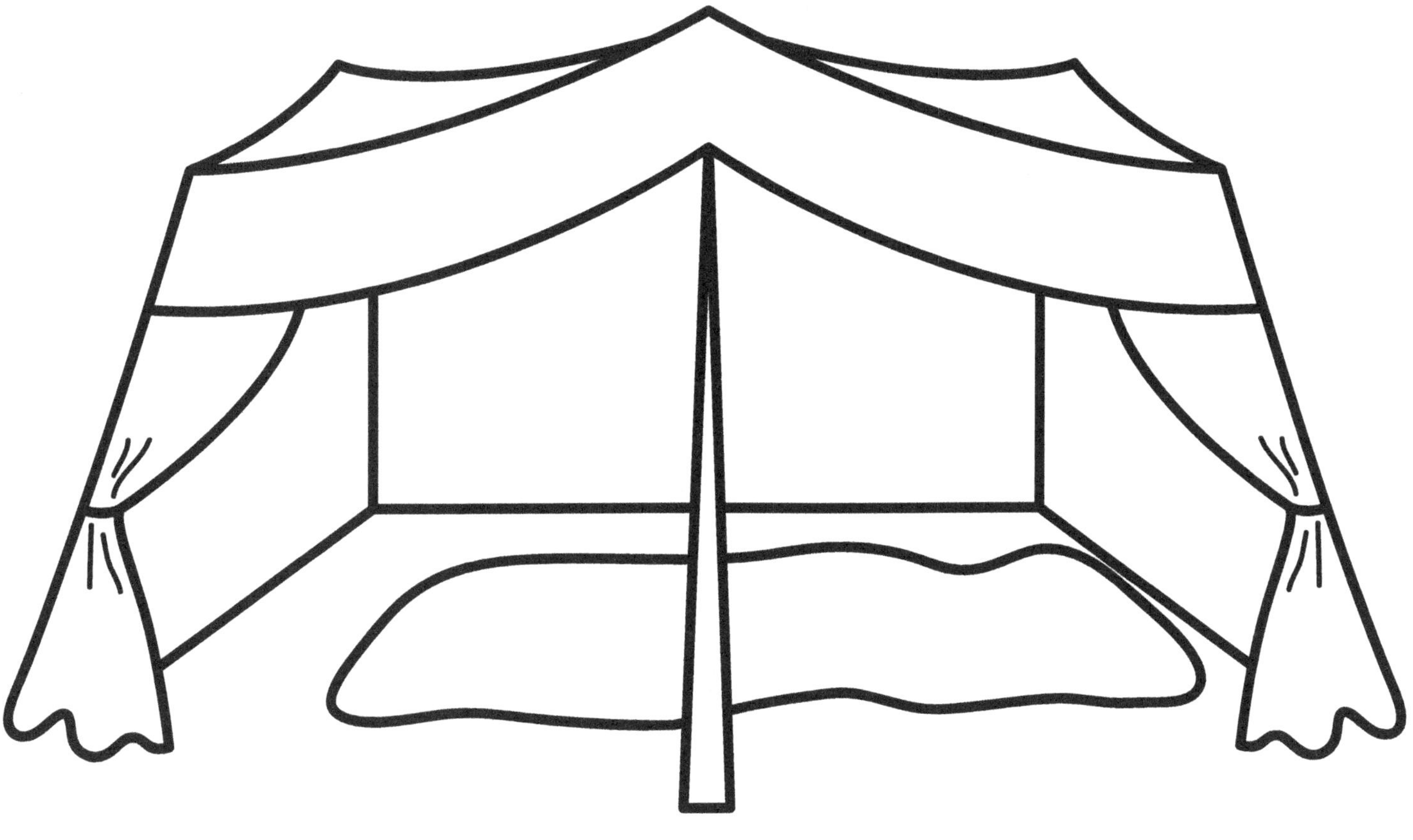

Israelite

Israelite

Israelite

Complete the pattern

Cut out the objects and place them in the correct box.

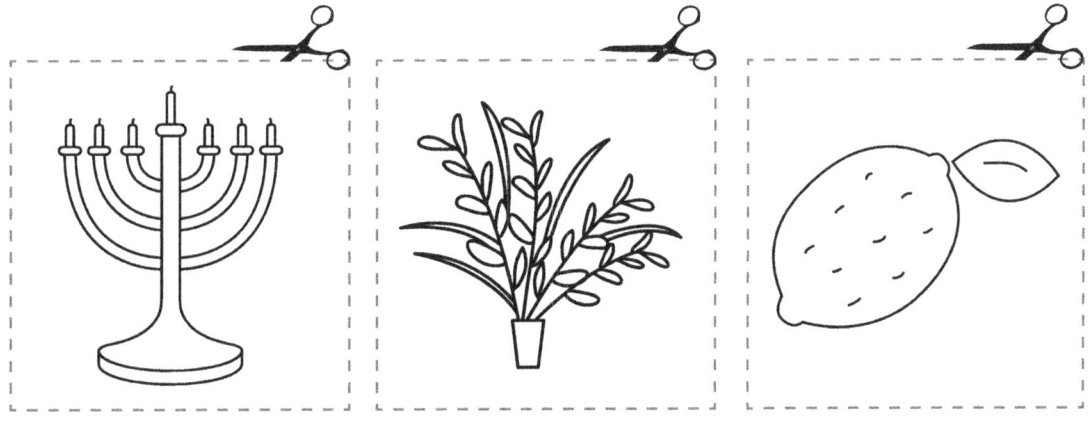

Grapes and olives

Grapes and olives were harvested at the time of Sukkot. Color and cut out the grapes and olives to fill up the bowl.

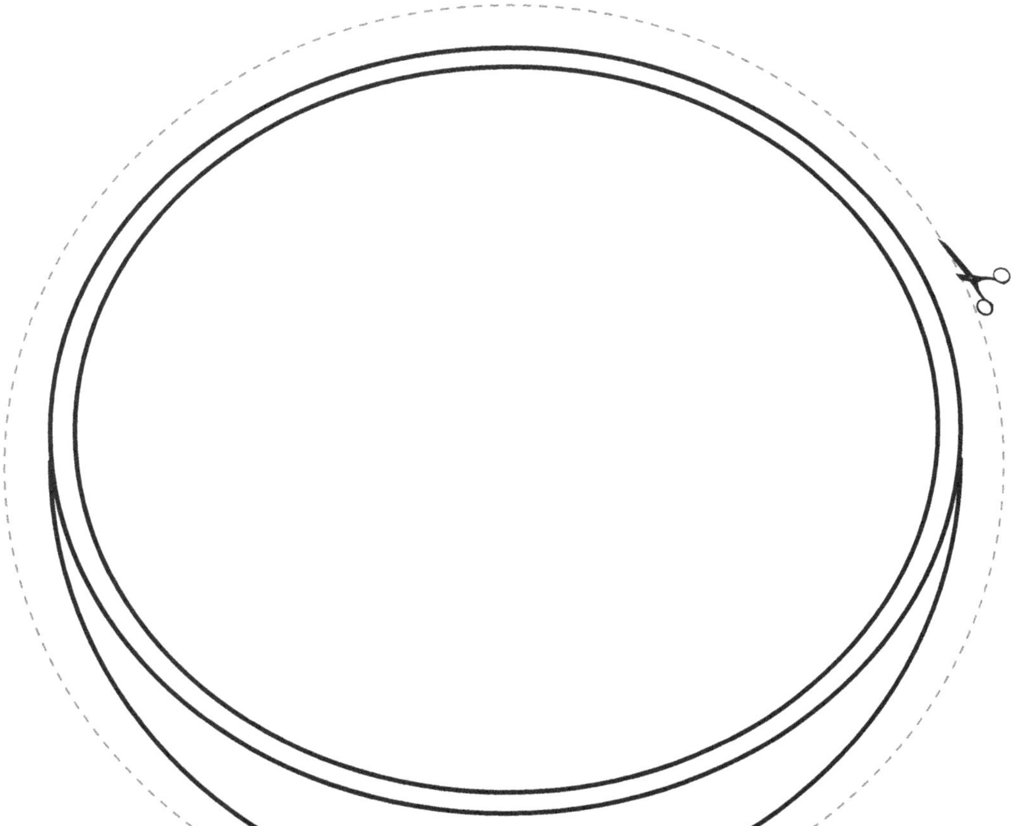

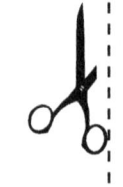

Sukkot flashcards

Color and cut out the flashcards.
Tape them around your home or classroom!

The water ceremony

During Sukkot, a priest took a jar of water from the pool of Siloam to use in the temple. Cut out the objects. Place them in the picture.

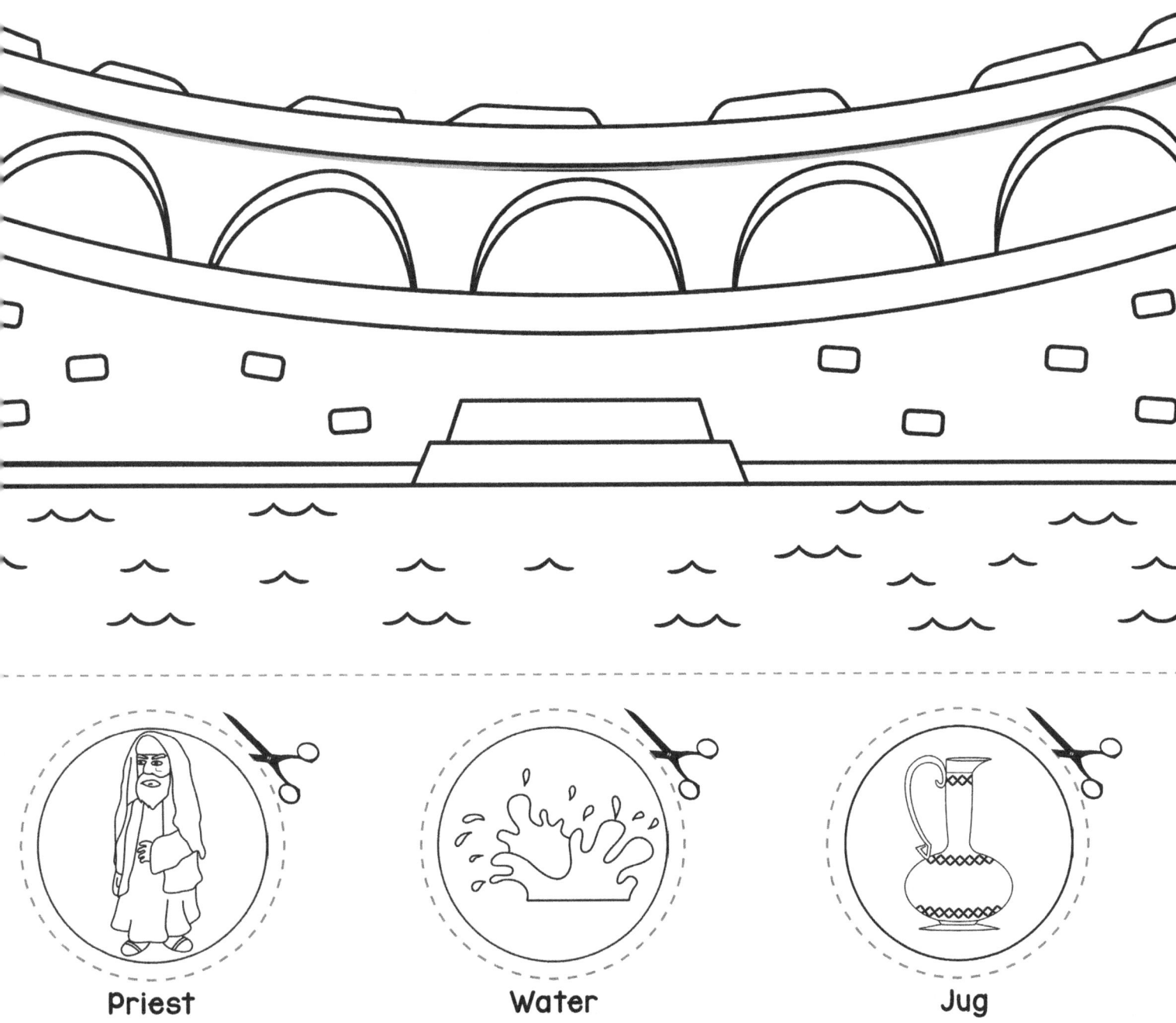

Priest   Water   Jug

Create a door hanger

You will need:
1. Heavy card stock or construction paper
2. Paint, felt pens, or crayons
3. Scissors (adult only)
4. Extra-strength glue sticks or tape

Instructions:

1. Paste the door hanger template page onto heavy card stock. Carefully cut out each template.
2. Ask your children to color the Fall Feasts circles. When they have finished, cut out and paste the circles onto the door hangers.
3. Make a reversible door hanger by pasting two templates together, back-to-back.
4. When the children have finished creating their door hangers, laminate or seal each door hanger using clear laminating sheets.

ta-da!

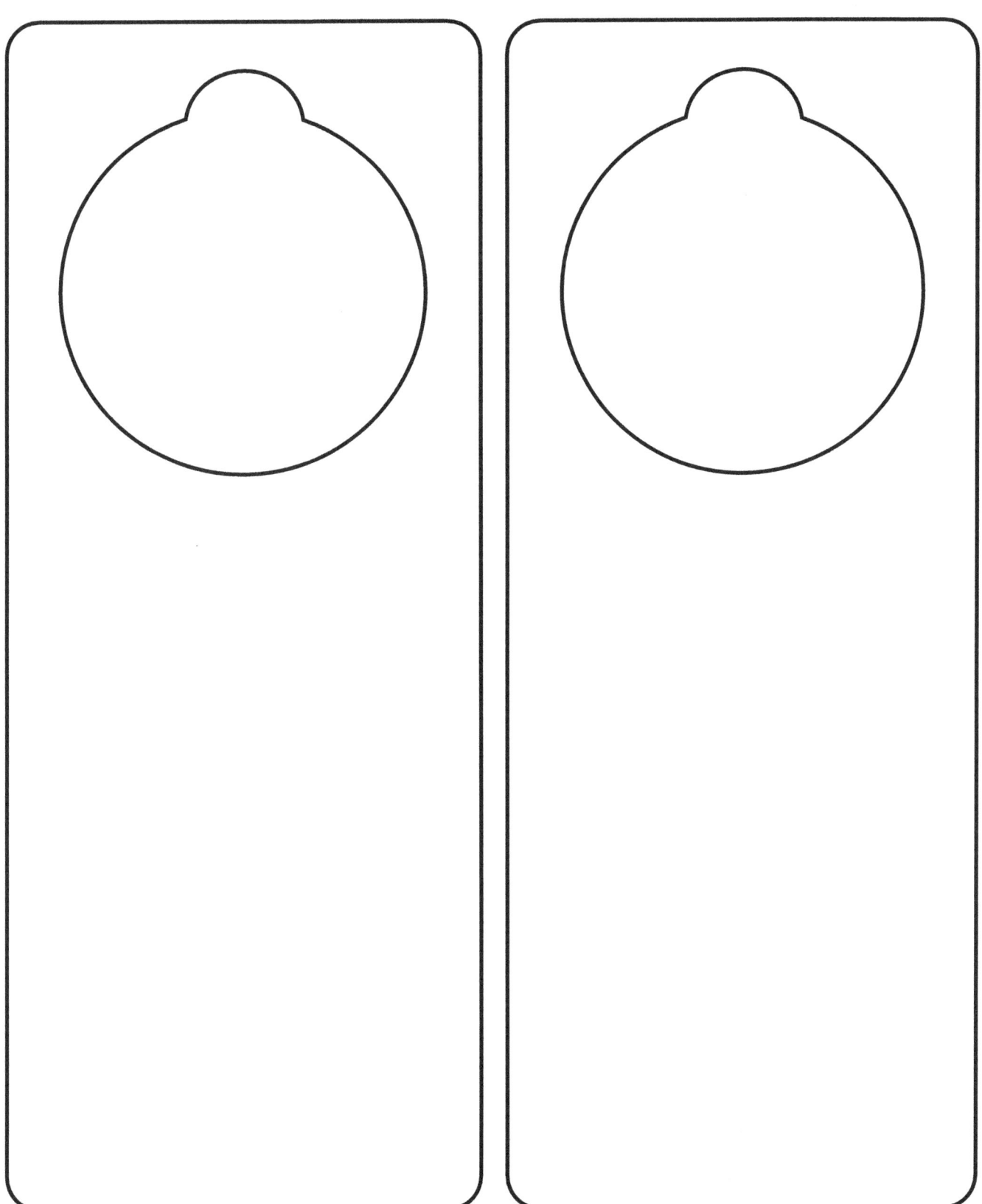

Discover more Activity Books!

Available for purchase at www.biblepathwayadventures.com

INSTANT DOWNLOAD!

The Spring Feasts
The Spring Feasts (Beginners)
The Fall Feasts
The Fall Feasts (Beginners)

Clean & Unclean (Beginners)
The Exodus (Beginners)
Moses Ten Plagues
Moses Ten Plagues (Beginners)

Made in the USA
Coppell, TX
01 September 2022